MW00778716

Yiddish for Babies

A Language Primer for Your Little *Pitsel*

WRITTEN AND ILLUSTRATED BY

JANET PERR

SIMON & SCHUSTER

New York   London   Toronto   Sydney

Simon & Schuster
1230 Avenue of the Americas
New York, NY 10020

First Simon & Schuster hardcover edition November 2009

SIMON & SCHUSTER and colophon are registered trademarks of
Simon & Schuster, Inc.

For information about special discounts for bulk purchases,
please contact Simon & Schuster Special Sales at
1-866-506-1949 or business@simonandschuster.com.

The Simon & Schuster Speakers Bureau can bring authors to your live event.
For more information or to book an event contact the Simon & Schuster Speakers
Bureau at 1-866-248-3049 or visit our website at www.simonspeakers.com.

Designed by Janet Perr and Kyoko Watanabe

Manufactured in the United States of America

10 9 8 7 6 5 4 3 2 1

Library of Congress Cataloging-in-Publication Data

Perr, Janet.
Yiddish for babies / Janet Perr.
p. cm.
1. Yiddish language—Humor. I. Title.

PN6231.J5P367 2009
439'.1864210207—dc22

ISBN 978-1-4391-5282-9
ISBN 978-1-4391-5621-6 (ebook)

For my baby, Jordan

Yiddish
for Babies

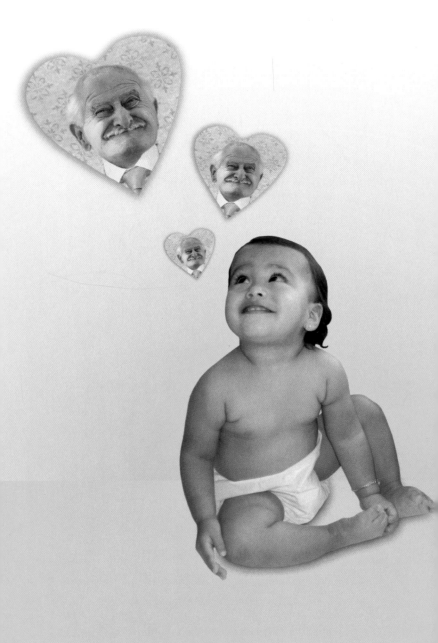

ALTER KOCKER

all•ter **kock**•er

grumpy old man

Baby loves her grandpa even though he's an **alter kocker.**

BUBBE

bu•bee

grandmother

Baby has so much fun when her **bubbe** comes to visit.

COCKAMAMIE

cock•a•may•mee

crazy

Baby! What are you doing with that **cockamamie** hat on your head?

DRECK
drek
garbage

Oy vey! Baby's sitting on a pile of **dreck.**

DREIDEL

dray•dull

a spinning top

Baby loves
watching the
dreidel spin.

FERKLEMPT

fur•**klempt**

emotional, ready to cry

It's naptime and baby's getting a little **ferklempt.**

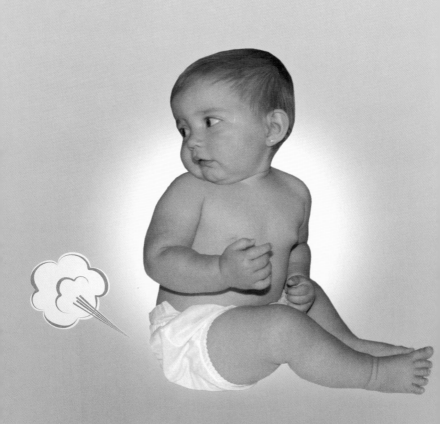

FORTZ
forts
fart

Ewww. Who made
that **fortz?**
It wasn't me!

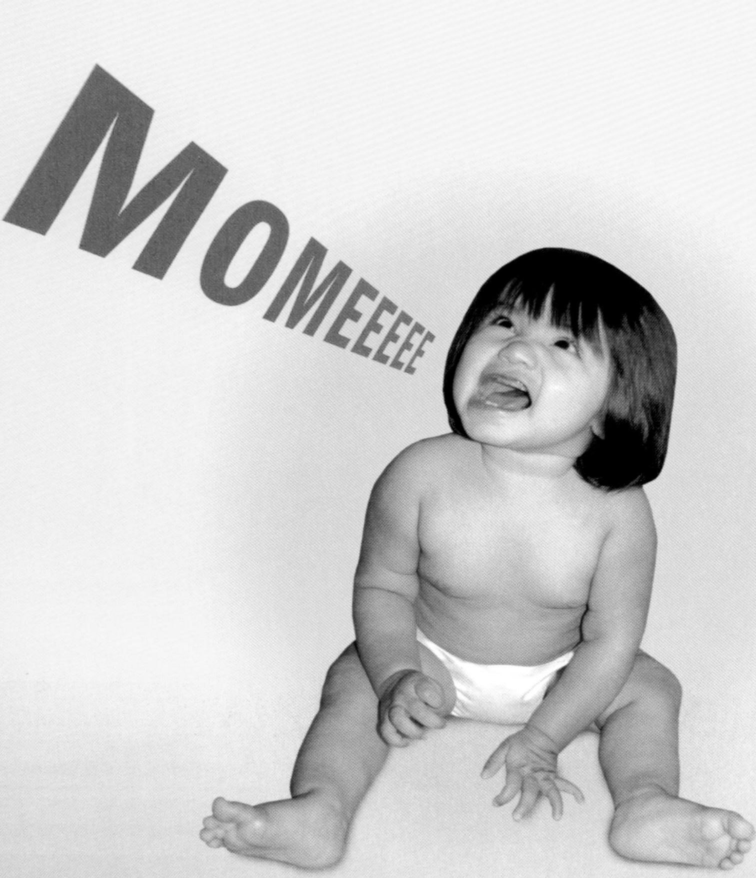
MOMEEEEE

GESHREI

geh•**shry**

scream

When baby calls for mommy, she lets out a big **geshrei.**

GONIFF

gah•nif

thief

Who stole the babka? Must be that little **goniff!**

KVELLING

kvel•ing

proud, bursting with joy

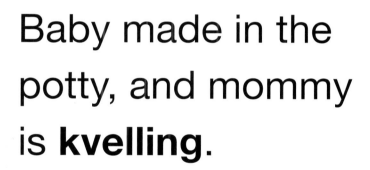

Baby made in the potty, and mommy is **kvelling**.

KVETCH
kvetch
complain

Stop **kvetching.**
Dinner will
be ready soon.

MEGILLAH

meh•**gill**•eh

a very long story

Wow, that's a big book and baby's reading the whole **megillah.**

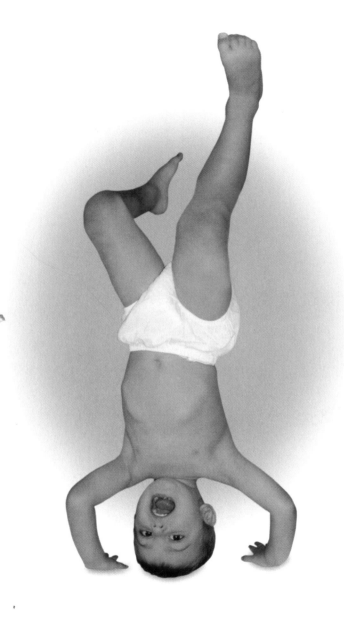

MESHUGGA

ma•**shu**•geh

crazy

Hey! What's baby doing? He's **meshugga.**

NOSH

nosh

snack

Mmm . . . baby's having a little **nosh** before bedtime.

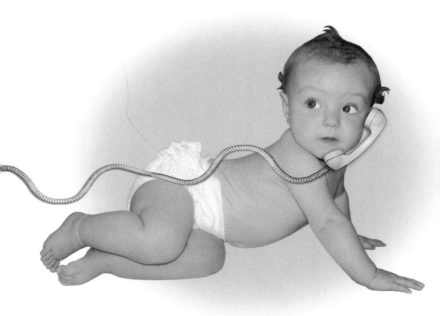

NU?
noo
so? well?

Nu? Did you hear we're having a playdate later? Yay!

ONGEPOTCHKET

oon•ge•potch•kit

gaudy, overdone

What a fancy baby, but she's way too **ongepotchket.**

OY GEVALT

oy ga•**valt**

uh-oh, oh no

Oy gevalt, baby spilled her milk!

PITSEL

pit•sul

a little bit

Baby loves petting her **pitsel** of a puppy. Gently, please!

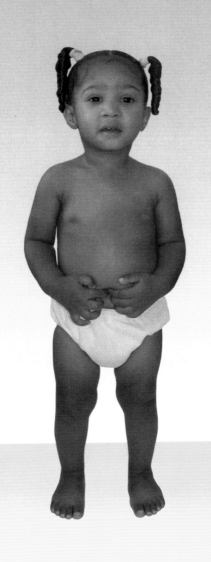

PUPIK

puh•pik

bellybutton

Where's your **pupik?** There it is!

SHAYNA MAIDEL

shay•nuh **may**•dull

pretty girl

My little **shayna maidel** likes to pose for the camera.

SHLUFFIN

shloof•en

sleeping

Shhhh, baby's finally resting. He'll be **shluffin** very soon.

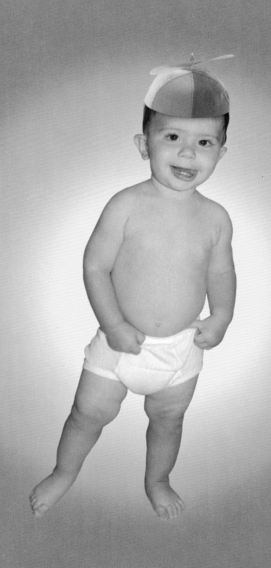

SHMENDRICK

shmen•drik

a silly boy

This **shmendrick**
is always making
funny faces.

SHMEAR
shmeer
a spread of some sort

Baby has a **shmear** of cream cheese with his lox and bagel.

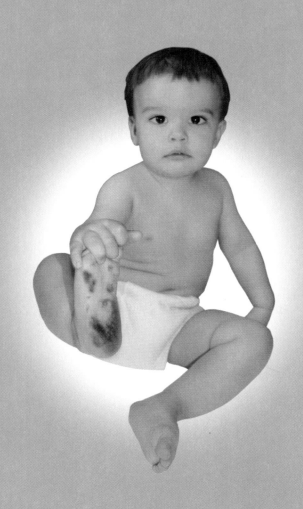

SHMUTZ

shmoots

dirt

Oy, fill up the tub.
Baby has **shmutz**
on his foot.

SHNOZZ

shnahz

a large nose

Silly baby! That's not your **shnozz.**

TRAIF

trayf

non-kosher food

Baby, why are you carrying around that **traif?**

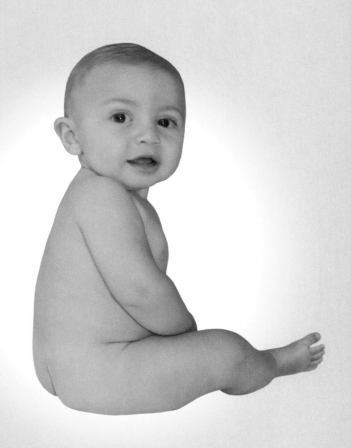

TUCHUS

took•us

tushy, bottom, hiney

Look! I see
baby's **tuchus!**

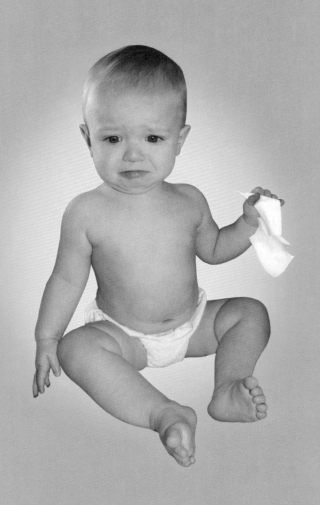

UNGABLOOZEN

oong•ga•blooz•en

sad, unhappy, pouting

Poor baby, she's **ungabloozen.** She misses mommy.

YIDDISHE KOP

yid•ish•a **cup**

smart person

Baby's on her way to Harvard. She's a real **yiddishe kop.**

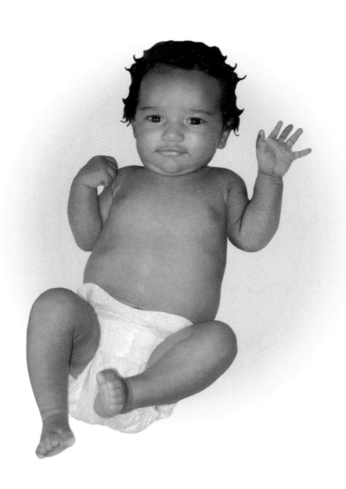

ZAI GEZUNT

zeye guh•**zoont**

be well, good-bye

Baby waves
bye-bye.
Zai gezunt!

ACKNOWLEDGMENTS

Special thanks to
David Rosenthal and Kerri Kolen
. . . you're the best!

And a kiss on the cheek to all of the
adorable babies I was able to put in this book.
I know your families are *kvelling*.